Pebble Plus

Science Tools

SCALES AND BALANCES

Lisa J. Amstutz

raintree
a Capstone company — publishers for children

Raintree is an imprint of Capstone Global Library Limited, a company incorporated in England and Wales having its registered office at 264 Banbury Road, Oxford, OX2 7DY – Registered company number: 6695582

www.raintree.co.uk
myorders@raintree.co.uk

Text © Capstone Global Library Limited 2020
The moral rights of the proprietor have been asserted.

All rights reserved. No part of this publication may be reproduced in any form or by any means (including photocopying or storing it in any medium by electronic means and whether or not transiently or incidentally to some other use of this publication) without the written permission of the copyright owner, except in accordance with the provisions of the Copyright, Designs and Patents Act 1988 or under the terms of a licence issued by the Copyright Licensing Agency, Barnard's Inn, 86 Fetter Lane, London, EC4A 1EN (www.cla.co.uk). Applications for the copyright owner's written permission should be addressed to the publisher.

Edited by Anna Butzer
Designed by Cynthia Della-Rovere
Picture research by Kelly Garvin
Production by Tori Abraham
Originated by Capstone Global Library Limited

ISBN 978 1 4747 6929 7 (hardback)
ISBN 978 1 4747 6947 1 (paperback)

British Library Cataloguing in Publication Data
A full catalogue record for this book is available from the British Library

Acknowledgements
We would like to thank the following for permission to reproduce photographs: Capstone Press/Karon Dubke: cover, 1, 7, 9, 13, 15, 17, 19, 21; iStockphoto/Moussa81, 3; Shutterstock: ben bryant, 11, paulaphoto, 5. Design elements: Shutterstock: Alina G, Astarina, Fafarumba, happy_fox_art, Lorelyn Medina, mhatzapa, Netkoff, Nikitina Karina, olllikeballoon, PedroNevesDesign, Visual Generation.

Every effort has been made to contact copyright holders of material reproduced in this book. Any omissions will be rectified in subsequent printings if notice is given to the publisher.

All the internet addresses (URLs) given in this book were valid at the time of going to press. However, due to the dynamic nature of the internet, some addresses may have changed, or sites may have changed or ceased to exist since publication. While the author and publisher regret any inconvenience this may cause readers, no responsibility for any such changes can be accepted by either the author or the publisher.

Printed and bound in India

Contents

Can you guess?................ 4
What is a balance?............. 6
What are scales?.............. 10
Let's measure!................ 16

Glossary................22
Find out more...........23
Websites...............23
Index..................24

Can you guess?

Pick up an apple and an orange. Which weighs more? You can guess. But to find out you need a tool.

What is a balance?

A balance can measure weight. It has two plates. One holds the item you want to weigh. The other holds weights.

A balance stands on a base.

A beam holds the two plates.

The beam can tilt from

side to side.

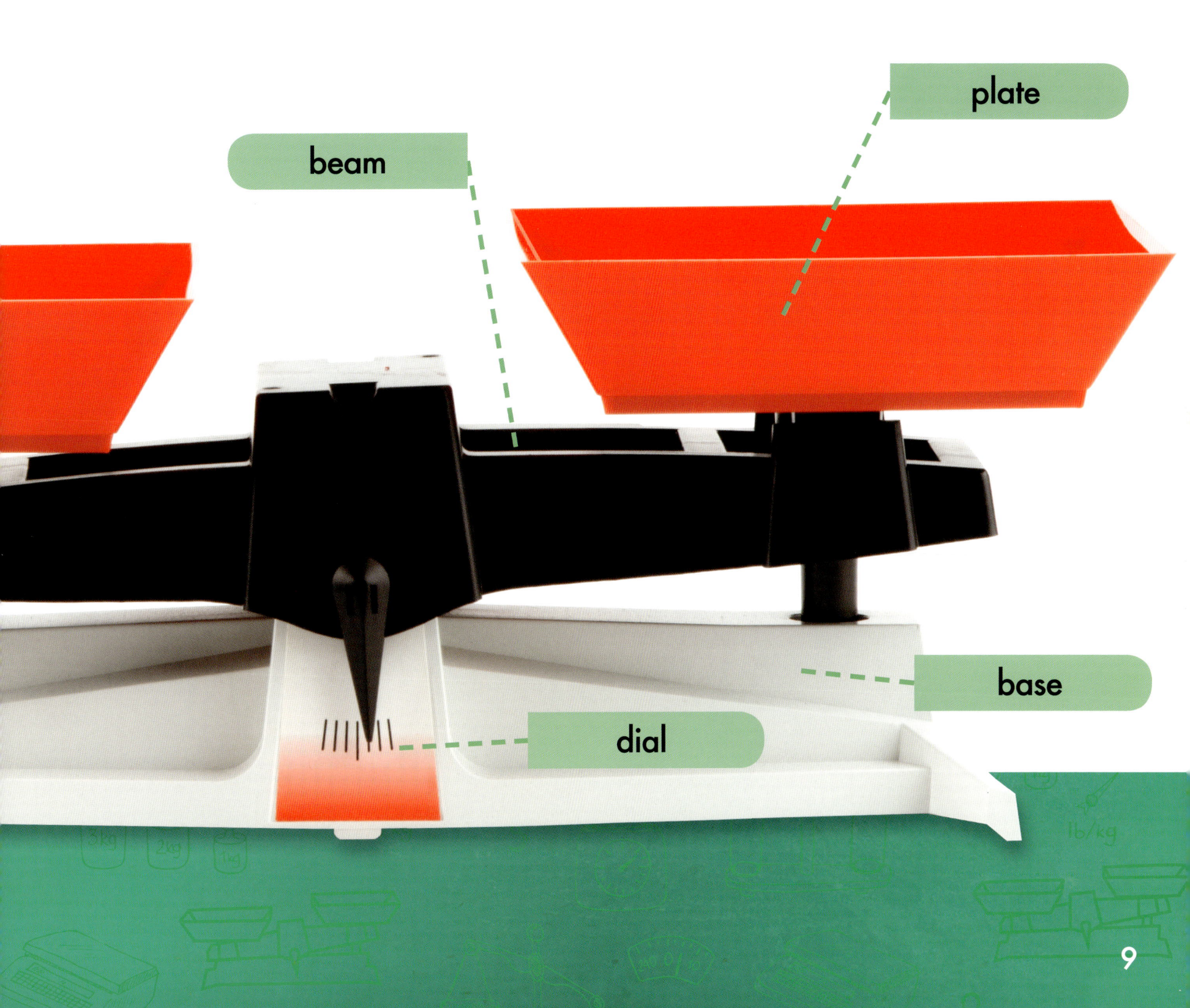

What are scales?

Scales measure weight.

Scales have a plate. Under the plate is a spring. The spring is pushed down. A dial measures the pressure.

Some scales measure in ounces and pounds. There are 16 ounces in 1 pound. A slice of bread weighs about 1 ounce. These 16 slices of bread weigh 1 pound.

Some scales are digital. They show the weight of an object on a small screen. Digital scales show different measures. These include grams and kilograms. There are 1,000 grams in 1 kilogram. Two paper clips weigh 1 gram.

digital scale

Let's measure!

Put an apple on one side of a balance. Put an orange on the other side. Which side is lower? Yes, the orange weighs more than the apple!

17

Put the apple on one of the plates. Place weights on the other plate until the plates are balanced. Add up the weights. That is the weight of the apple.

19

Measure the apple's weight with a scale. Put the apple on the scale. Read the number on the dial. The apple weighs 227 grams (8 ounces).

Glossary

beam a straight piece of plastic or metal that holds the cups or pans of a balance

gram a unit of metric weight measurement; there are 1,000 grams in 1 kilogram

kilogram a unit of metric weight measurement

measure to find out the size of something

ounce a unit of weight; 1 ounce is 28 grams

pound a unit of weight; there are 16 ounces in 1 pound

pressure the force made by pressing on something

spring a tightly twisted piece of metal that can be squeezed or stretched but always returns to its former shape

tool something used to make work easier

weight a measurement of how heavy something is

Find out more

How to Measure Everything: A Fun First Guide to the Maths of Measuring, DK (DK Children, 2018)

Master Maths Book 3: Measure Up (Length, Weight, Size and Capacity), Anjana Chatterjee (QED Publishing, 2018)

Using a Scale (Super Science Tools), Nora Roman (Gareth Stevens Publishing, 2017)

Websites

DK Findout! Weight and mass
www.dkfindout.com/us/science/forces-and-motion/weight-and-mass/

Maths is Fun: metric mass
www.mathsisfun.com/measure/metric-mass.html

Index

balance 6, 8, 16, 18

grams 14

kilograms 14

measuring 6, 10, 12, 14, 16, 18, 20

ounces 12, 20

plate 6, 8, 10, 16, 18

pounds 12

scales 10, 12, 14, 20

spring 10

weights 6, 18